Sammie
and the New Baby

Written By
Sue Gilligan-Hannon

Illustrated By
Morgan Spicer

Sammie and the New Baby

ISBN 978-1-7359614-0-8

For Mom, Kevin, Aiden, Sean and
of course, Sammie and Lulu

Hi! My name is Sammie. I'm a **Goldendoodle.**

I live with my family and I have a great life.

I like to go on long walks with my daddy, and...

I **LOVE** to eat!

I like to go for rides in the car with my mommy, and...

I like to play with my family, and...

I **LOVE** to eat!

I like to sit outside in the sun, and... I **LOVE** to eat!

Did I mention that I love to **EAT**?
I love food, food, food!

I love my family and they love me!

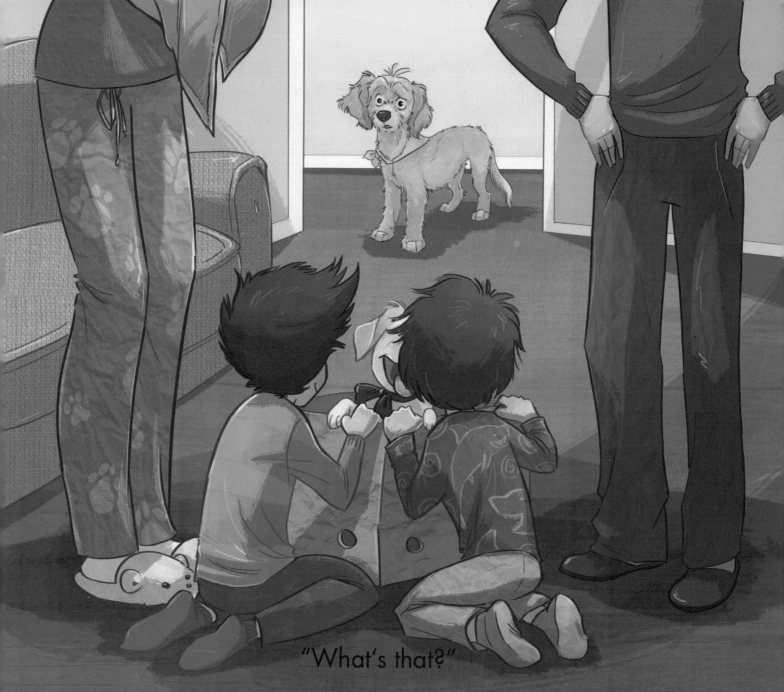

"What's that?"

"Don't worry, Sammie. Everything's going to be okay!"

Yay! Nana and Pop are here...

I LOVE Pop! He always plays with me
and scratches my belly.

"Hey, look at me! Over here!

...Yoo-hoo!
Remember me?"

"**Lulu** is our brand-new baby, **Sammie**. Be gentle!"

It's nighttime and everyone should be sleeping.

Why are
they awake?

"Wait! Isn't
that my bed?"

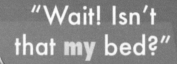

"You go back to sleep, Sammie. Don't worry.
Everything's going to be okay!"

Is everything going to be okay?

About the Author

Sammie and the New Baby is Sue Gilligan-Hannon's first of a series of books featuring her **goldendoodles**, Sammie and Lulu. Sue's mission, with the help of her beloved dogs, is to assist parents and children navigate the struggles that come with early childhood.

Besides being a dog lover, Sue is an avid volunteer, a social media marketing expert, and an advocate for gun violence prevention. She lives in northwestern New Jersey.

CPSIA information can be obtained
at www.ICGtesting.com
Printed in the USA
BVHW020907220221
600764BV00003B/16